Copyright © 2023 by Dian Brand

All rights reserved. No part of this book may be reproduced or transmitted in any form or by any means without permission in writing from the publisher.

www.innovatorspioneers.com

Innovators and Pioneers

Estée Lauder

Written by Diane Z.
Illustrated by Natalia Larguier

Josephine Esther Mentzer was born in Queens, New York. Her friends liked to call her Esty, and later in life, she changed her name to Estée with a cool French accent. This is her incredible story about passion, beauty, and love.

Estée loved beauty from a very young age. She enjoyed brushing her mom's long hair and putting creams on her face to make her look and feel special.

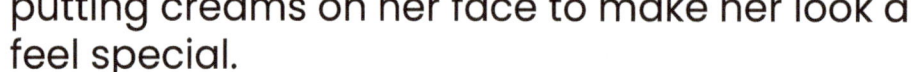

Estée grew up watching her uncle concoct wonderful creams in the kitchen. She learned cream's magical power to make people beautiful.

Estée dreamed of delivering beauty to everyone in the world one day.

At a young age, Estée worked at her family's hardware store. She learned that sales were not just about selling things, but also about listening to and helping people.

Later on, Estée found love in Joseph Lauder, a kind and supportive man who believed in her dreams.

They became a team, helping each other through the ups and downs of life. Later on, they had two wonderful boys, Leonard and Ronald.

Being good was never enough for Estée.

Estée got her start by selling her products in beauty salons.

She believed that to make a sale, Estée needed to touch the customer, talk to the customer, and teach the customer how to use her products.

Estée aspired to share her beauty products with more people, and wanted her products to be available in the major department stores. At first, they all said no, but she didn't give up.

Estée aspired to share her beauty products with more people, and wanted her products to be available in the major department stores. At first, they all said no, but she didn't give up.

Around this time, Estée used her creativity and came up with a clever idea: give free gifts along with her products. The concept of "gift with purchase" turned out to be so successful that everyone began to do it.

Product packaging was very important to Estée. She visited many customers' bathrooms to ensure the packaging would match customers' wallpapers, and convey a sense of harmony and luxury.

Before Estée, most women reserved fancy perfumes for special occasions. But Estée had a brilliant idea to give every woman a wonderful, yet affordable fragrance, so she created a unique bath oil called "Youth-Dew".

As time went by, Estée became a respected icon in the beauty industry. She proved that women can be powerful business leaders.

This earned her lots of loyal customers and new friends, including some of the most influential celebrities and royalty.

Estée was loved by people from all around the world. She didn't only focus on her business, but also had a big heart for helping others. She worked for charities and gave all the love back to the world.

Estée's magical products made people feel beautiful inside and out. She always believed in the power of women and said, "Be aware of your boundless potential."

Her beauty empire continued to grow until this day, making the world a more beautiful place for everyone to enjoy.

www.ingramcontent.com/pod-product-compliance
Lightning Source LLC
Chambersburg PA
CBHW061406010526
44119CB00011B/273